LOWERCASE GOD

LOWERCASE GOD

Poems by Mark Fleckenstein

Grateful acknowledgement to the editors of the following
publications where some of these poems first appeared:

— *Cimarron Review*: "Last Photograph of my Days as an
  Idealist"
— *Slant*: "Foreign Movie"

Attention schools and businesses: for discounted copies on large
orders, please contact the publisher directly.

For information contact:
Unsolicited Press
Portland, Oregon
www.unsolicitedpress.com
orders@unsolicitedpress.com
619-354-8005

Cover Design: Kathryn Gerhardt
Editor: Kristen Marckmann ; S.R. Stewart
ISBN: 978-1-956692-24-2

If you call it God, then it is God. God is whatever God allows.
—Don Deillo, **The Falling Man**

The poet remains divorced from the uppercase God
—Jonathan Galassi, "Reading Montale"

Contents

For Mary Veazey

LAST PHOTOGRAPH OF MY DAYS AS AN IDEALIST

You urge me, after so many years of silence, to send you details about my occupations, about this "wonderful" world in which, you say, I am lucky enough to live and move and have my being. I might answer that I am a man without occupation, and that this world is not in the least wonderful.

—E.M. Cioran, "Letter To A Faraway Friend"

How far I have come to wish
to come home. This morning,
the first in twenty-three
exiled years, the white noise
of commerce eclipsed my only dream
of childhood: the dull boots
and swollen faces of bodies hang-
ing from streetlamps. Your letters
and wishes for my life here
arrive whitened by a belief
in this country like a trinket
of light perfect and invisible.
What has not changed and what
has are identical. 28 years earlier,
Chinese tanks and soldiers rolled
over students. Here whole families
sleep on sewer grates and barter

for whatever one might spare.
Yesterday, a pigeon appeared on
my desk and pecked at your letters.
My cat caught it in mid-flight.
The argument of its wings
surprised him into letting it go.

SONG FOR FIVE VOICES

I.

Night falls like a tree in the suburbs.
Newly washed lawn,

the welcoming sidewalk to a locked door.
Small luminous utterances.

Pants like a wall in mid-fight.

II.

A calm anger has carried me thus far
like a boat against the breeze.

What more could I want? Snail shell,
you must carry me and this world.

Shirt colored an imagined light.

III.

Numbers, not zeros, reliable as rocks.
If making a family, there's where to start.

But no longer. Beginnings falter in ensuing years.
Lack strength, compassion, memory.

Shoes like revenge for having walked three steps.

IV.

Several hours beyond sleep and rain. Past tall
grass pastures, hills variously colored

pastoral and sweet air. Then one thump, two thump,
hard thump, hurt thump thump thump.

Hair like the imagined life of a child.

V.

An extravagant, raw charm. If colored at all, red.
Deep and sensual, not bloodied.

A song like that could save a building, improve
weather. The singer growing lighter.

Voice like burned letters.

DREAMS

Last night's rain fixed nearly everything:
streets smoothed again black,

plants thankful and sated, the house again
able to settle. And while I slept,

the sheets whispered over my dreams,
retouching and torching the details,

squaring knots, truing the blanks.

PRAYER FOUND IN AN ABANDONED MONESTARY

Water. Sunned hair, rotted wood. Winter
like a folded blanket. All the windows quieted.

Two chairs. Broken only by light, a table, absent plates.
A prayer stalled against the knuckles.

Please let me come home.

There was a door, the wrong night's stars,
inconspicuous music. Not really winter.

Almost green. There was no more.
Only your voice. And our talk.

Not God, not now, no. And where.

I am wary of you. A liquid presence, but human, solid.
Breath and breath. Breathe as breathe, mostly.

House and barn, weather's argument.
Words, words, worlds.

Another? Rapture, ruptured, bedeviled blue.

FOREIGN MOVIE

7:05 a.m.

Light and loose change strewn
into the folds and shadows of the room.
A radio saxophone floating above the static.
His voice slams her eyes shut.
An overcoat flies out the door.

7:51 a.m.

Commuter cars, trains and buses cough
to a dead stop. Horns like saxophone notes
climb through the clouds and inside offices
where coffee breakfasts compete
with the telephone's whine for attention.

8:08 a.m.

Passing a saxophone player while rushing
to work, his melody turns familiar.
Over a non-business lunch of white wine

and intimate talk with a close friend,
The name of the song forgotten.

6:17 p.m.

He will fix her a perfect dinner:
Lobster. Fresh vegetables. French wine.
And something exotic for dessert. Will
soothe her mood with dining room candles,
one white rose and soft saxophone music.

No, I don't know whatever happened
to them. They left this album –
it was their favorite – behind
when they moved.
It's some saxophone player

FIRST BABY PICTURES

Before birth, blood-music and breathing errors,
yellowed light. The heart's muscular thinking,
short-fisted and shallow. The picture is gray-
focused, startled inexactly, dulled to ordinary.
What it is saying, is equally hopeful and hopeless.

HANDFUL OF DUST

The light was monstrous. Pristine,
cut, suffused perfect. His mind gravel.
What if God was the next room?
The color wood and glass turn.
Straw-drawn respiration. These are his hands.

THE ART OF MEMORY

Warm dark. Blinds penciled against windows
ignorant of light and other grammars. The walls,
nearer words, breath, motion. The hands,
articulate if only almost. The door, by presence
and appearance, must mean something

SELF PORTRAIT WITH CAT AND SLEEPING CHILDREN

The room parses sleep, silence, darkness, soiled murmurs.
A nearby river talks to itself passing, not unlike rain
but more certainly, but there is no rain. To move
would require glass, aimed breath to holds its place, wind.
There is no wind. The air outside wishes to stay there.

SELF PORTRAIT: TURNING 49

Clear sky thunder, a cloudless blue wrinkle
of noise like forgotten company. Otherwise, nothing
is provoked. Forgetful light, ambivalent heat, air damaged
voices, not intended for windows, the embrace of grass.
If I could be anywhere, I would be. And why not.

TRAVEL ADVISORY

Some days the world is a luscious peach.
Others, a cold boiled potato. The difference
between knowing what to do and doing it
is four dollars. How you get there is your business.
If praying your way, lock the door after you leave.

SELF PORTRAIT WITH IMAGINARY ANGEL

You see, you can live without having survived.
                    —Carolyn Forche, from *"The Blue Hour"*

What he would, what will, and what.
Talking and making talk, literal —

always words, indecorous colors: Blue varying —
sometimes, hard coaxed red, blackened purple.

As if made by God to tear wings from angels.

SLEEP TALK

Night-flecked windows. Stars crimp across
misshapen blinds. Shadows snore like bats.
      Unfettered
mirrors dream bodies, smudged,
        and sound-colored.

This is the only world. There could be others
quite the same, as ravished, as unremarkably red
        gone red.

SEMANTICS

For the want of particulars—
God, sledgehammer, hummingbird, cellar door,
I let go,
        loosening the difference between name
  and object.
The day like a balloon robbed of air, sun torn.

I remember.

IMAGINED SCARS

White-slit straight,
blood-taped, bandaged. To itself, red-aged, sharp

to the mind, the touch-thought imaged, marooned.
       A strand.
A thought thought. Near the sink, swimming. Red.

Hesitant, deliberate pauses. Any sharp edges' way
       of breathing.

COFFEE SHOP

It's wrong for you not to know how beautiful
you are, your eyes, dark haired stories,

secrets like red shoes. Or walking, your wings
perceptible, just. Budding, fine.

Finally ready, rising, to love, to the air.

THE MEMORY IN ABSENCE

White shirts, white light.
Laughter like coarse fur rubbed
against faces. A door. Some boxes.

Light like spilled milk. Click.
And where were you.

DIPTYCH

I. Memory

If she remembers him, the evening stars
and moon are out early.

Remembers hair. Light bled sheets.
Stories stretching from room to room.

What does this remind you of?
The photograph of strangers

relaxed poolside in Florida.
Bodies, large, fish belly white.

Arms incapable of embrace

2. Object of Memory

Her voice became the only place
he spent time and laughed.

Made love to it when staring out
at muted neighborhood lights.

With the right tools and enough
patience, could make it a mirror.

Maybe tomorrow

SELF PORTRAIT WITH THE RADIO ON

Last night I might have had Retsina
and not cut myself shaving before bed
had it not been for wishing to be elsewhere,
goaded by the mirror to hurry, to clear
its view of the room. Tonight
will end much the same: watching
a woman's hands pretend to know
the piano keys, wishing to be fixed
inside the song. When you visit
the Oracle, it's best to have your question
in mind as well as written on your hand.
While a live rabbit or lamb might travel
better than a statue, both are necessary
forms of appreciation. The spoils
of conquest or dumb luck, too.
Laid against itself, notated in
the player's and composer's mind,
shadow becoming shadow and back
again, to solid. The after-effect,
peripatetic, multiphasic. If watered
into bloom, again in the room, a hand
coaxing a hand to become real.
This could be the thing that lasts;
Makes physical, thought. Is this
how to remember? This could
be the things that lasts.

COMMENTARY

Coming back again. Fully loaded. Trying to again remember what something smelled like. Michigan, the furious September snow. Giddy streetlights, fireflies and moving. The house, a series of boxes labeled *Kitchen, Living Room, Den, Bedroom.* Days fail me. I wonder for God, if he listens, to what music. I know somewhere I am happy. This is what's missing.

FROM THE FILM "THE RED SHOES"

He wonders after her, the performance of her absence,
present. Wrinkled air, light
as a drinking glass anticipating water,
mixed conversation, the residue of how her red shoes
explained her.

RECONSTRUCTING SLEEP

If he wonders, it is sleep.
Night, brass stars, the quiet pounding
of traffic somewhere. Imagines how
she might sleep, her hands having
danced all day, talk quietly. Constructs what meaning feels,
tries to find where she might, how to right
       a frayed knot.

SOMETIMES A RED SHOE IS JUST A RED SHOE

I

From where I wasn't to now,
it's the same damn river twice two times over
and clear enough for the rocks to recognize
the color yellow and what it means.
If they wandered closer, we'd be friends.
Everything is water if you wait long enough.

II

From where he wasn't to now, his life is untrue.
His days are instructions from accidents.
A river twice the same. The rocks learned
how to recognize the color yellow
and what it means. If they wandered closer,
they'd be his friends.

Instructions from accidents, his life is untrue,
his days twice the same, a river. From where
he wasn't to now, the rocks learned

they'd be friends. How to recognize the color
yellow, what it means. And that if you
wait long enough, everything is water.

"THE RED SHOES WILL NOT PERFORM TONIGHT"

The act of her anger, of
the anger she felt then
not turning to him

—Robert Creeley, from "Goodbye"

She sits not as knowing. *The red shoes*
will not perform tonight. The blood rage,
a room of familiar music calculates flesh
meaning not words, but gestures: a hand
sewn to teeth, what she could.
A question, emotional and arguing,
          between what and what.

THE HOUSE SLEEPS

Night lightens its embrace of windows
as first light tinsels the last stars.
Her dark hair, free to her shoulders, pauses.
The house exhales and is gentle at her.
He sleeps, rumpled and dream
sodden. Wanting what the other knows.

The light is always burned out even
by morning. What he would and what he can duel
over his coffee. He remembers her brevity against
him, the wind unable to swim between them,
knowing whatever might happen already had.

IMAGING CHICAGO

He tried to embrace a moon
In the Yellow River.

—Ezra Pound, from "Epitaphs"

The moon
overlaid with frost, star-bled ghost-clouds.
Spidery, silk-black and warm to the eye, unsullied
breathing, dream-calmed, she lay. He thinks of her
as where. Maybe wrongly. Affectionate trouble, his.
Pennies for opened eyes.

SOLO PRAYER

A mishandled compliment, awkward wakened
desire. The sixth degree of fondness.
Prayer beads fingered, slowly articulated
dust, murmuring, rote. A mirror.
The last penny in its pocket.

THREE YEARS ON

Balanced. As if as wanting
wanted. What they would
make, what don't.
What if a window?
Story-curtain? Boiled-down stars?
      Dancing for memory.

WINTER IN THIRTEEN LINES

The telephone is wary of this chilled room,
windows flirting wintry. There are words
for this: blistered, frothy another
room's conversation. The light is faulty.
In another room, a chair waits like a dog.
There were foot echoes, smells, even
breathing coinciding with motion, an arm
straightening emotion, calculating what texture
or color makes sense or real, the thing the hand
would neaten. To best explain longing: the sun,
even shining, is a cold pastel, clouds visibly blue,
pretending to be gray, and ambivalent, come
harshly. The room, a hole in the roof,
        listens anxiously.

ALIKE AS THEY ARE NOT

A relationship. *If he, if she, if they...*
Fleshy dialogue between a body

and a body. An attenuated moment. Just air.
Hand cast. Pure as art. Plastic thought,

grammatical statuary. Pleasure, nearly chess-like.

.

ICONOGRAPHY

In hell the angels sing too.

—Gregory Corso

Heaven lacks music. Fog-smudged voices
eviscerate blood-harmonies. Ghost notes,
amelodic, atonal, pornographic, contrapuntal.
Not *Abandon all hope, ye who enter,* rather
It's your hell you burn in it. The fields, green,
plentiful, and always greener than here.

STILL LIFE, WINTER LIT

Clouds like crows. Swollen like overcoats. Asking
for a window, a mirror-sliver, my heart
thumpboot thumpboot thumpboot
thumpboot, embarrassed by desire,
its half-twin. A perfect syllogism: all circles and touching,
      explained into place.

DIALECTIC

If it is to be true that a man is not in despair, one must
annihilate the possibility every instant.
                    —Soren Kierkegaard, *The Sickness Unto Death*

A fooled moon, folded
between clouds. Ratted out. Once again
his statue kneels or tries to kneel. A prayer
gripped by the neck and shoulders.
A demiurge. Discarded and drowned at least twice.

OCTOBER ELEGY

Snow begat mountains. Iron white sky, houses
fenced, cold lit. Clouds torn dark, air torn by hand,
near prayer, near fist, near. If she leans, it is in.
Not falling, held, loved. There is no other.
No either, no not. As the day empties its pockets,
one star falls up, flowers warm as night begins.

A NEW YEAR

One erasing day the others follow, curious
as to where. Eurydice's call to Orpheus
on the way down, her song.

STREETLIGHT ECLIPSE

After 2 am, milk-stars, A singed moth's ecstatic
death-flight. Icarus, Earhart, *Enola Gay.*

Knowledge
means loss, purity. A full winter full moon,
      the eighteenth enigma,
compliments, complicates decisions. Visible breath,
      windows, another.

CRETE, 1993

Zeus, in the form of a bull with a saffron crocus,
seduced Europa. Not gently, not without
tenderness, even joy.

His whiteness. Beautifully hideous. Her love,
unmistakable, unremarkable like white marble.

At night, veined shards rise like stars, mistaking
voices for flowers.

PRAYER: RESCINDING

Dear Friend—You are like God. We pray to Him, & He
answers "No." Then we pray to Him to rescind the "No,"
He don't answer at all
    —Emily Dickinson, from a letter written in the summer of 1883

I.

I paint days and stars where there are stars,
and dark, what would be the moon.
I borrow loose colors, unfaithful light, unbruised prayers—
like strands of pearls.
Ideal? *No*—Just the stars.

2.

Letters christened, circumspect, innocent, stamped
Return To Sender. Indelicately handled, embarrassed.
Friend — not God—*answer.* Please. I wait. Days
unfold, room by emptied room.
Fields of dwarf marigolds, *flores de la muerte*, call.

ETYMOLOGY

I

Ill-tempered blue sky and one undressed window
dissolve into mathematics: two glassed shadows,

two chairs, a table and anxiety. *Explain what's
missing.* your face, the grace of your moving,

in and against time, quieting away.
The future humming, *I will hate you.*

2.

One person equals an obsession; two, a passion...
(from the Latin passionem (nom. passio)

"suffering, enduring") Two years of left over stars
later, generations of long dead trick-light,

still traveling, equally real, unreal, hope colored.

.

LOOKING—GLASS

Gray minded, eased into thinking
like hands, troubling for words.
Jaw, temples, cheek bones, eye-bays mimic a face.

Your ghost, a room owed a face. Boarded up windows,
        warped doors.
No looking glass for a moment, water thin.

NO ONE COMES OUT ALIVE

Inexactly consolable, as if
lain together, her shoulder, back, legs untouched but near. Paused.

Words, worlds. A spider's cloth. The delicacy, thin
strength, pure and made so. An obvious wisdom.

Him? All art is failure.

.

SELF PORTRAIT IN LATE SPRING

Three crows in an evening field own
the dulled translation of green

toward shadow, wind and thinking:
trees, next week, what do you mean?

A shift in wings, flight like held breath.

Author Bio

Mark Fleckenstein was born in Chicago, and grew up in Ohio, Michigan, Connecticut, North Carolina, and New Hampshire. He graduated from University of North Carolina in Charlotte with a B.A. in English, Vermont College of Fine Arts and received an MFA in Writing. He's became very involved in the poetry community in and around Boston, for over 30 years. He was an assistant editor for (BLuR), the *Boston Literary Review*, founder/coordinator of two bi-weekly poetry reading series in Boston and a workshop leader, He's given poetry readings with famous poets (Charles Simic, Linda Gregg, Mark Doty, Mark Cox and Carl Phillips) and not so famous poets. Six states and dozens of moves later, he settled in Massachusetts. He is also a painter. He has two amazing daughters and an large, eccentric, long-haired black cat named Ariadne.

Notes

"From The Film, *Red Shoes* ," "Reconstructing Sleep,"
"Sometimes A Red Shoe Is Just A Red Shoe," "Wet Street With
Red Shoes," "*The Red Shoes Will Not Perform Tonight,*"
"Soliloquy For One Shoe And The Color Red," "The House
Sleeps," "Imaging Chicago," "Solo Prayer," "Three Years On," and
"Winter In Thirteen Lines" are for g.

"October Elegy" is for Jere Griffiths

"Crete, 1993" is for Karen Bjorkman

"Coffee Shop" is for Vivian Cucchiara

"Prayer Found In An Abandoned Monastery" is for Cat Smith.

—

"No One Comes Out Alive" the last line is taken from Richard
Hugo's *The Triggering Town: Lectures and Essays on Poetry and
Writing* (Norton, 1979)

www.ingramcontent.com/pod-product-compliance
Lightning Source LLC
Chambersburg PA
CBHW031255120626
46545CB00007B/2831